*Manganese*

ROBERT SAXTON was born in Nottingham in 1952 and now lives in north London, where he is the editorial director of an illustrated book publishing company. His first collection of poetry, *The Promise Clinic*, was published by Enitharmon Press in 1994. He is also represented in Faber's *Poetry Introduction 7* and the Carcanet/Oxford*Poets* anthology *Oxford Poets 2001*. In 2001 he won the Keats–Shelley Memorial Association's poetry prize for 'The Nightingale Broadcasts'.

Also by Robert Saxton

*The Promise Clinic*

For
Allan, Irene,
Duncan and Ewan

# Acknowledgements

Thanks are due to the editors of the following publications in which some of these poems first appeared:

*Bridge of Stars* and *Life Lines* (Duncan Baird Publishers), *Exeter Poetry Prize Anthology 1999* (Odyssey Press), *Keats–Shelley Review 2001*, *Metre*, *New Writing Three* (Minerva), *Oxford Magazine*, *Oxford Poets 2001* (Carcanet/Oxford*Poets*), *PN Review*, *Poetry London*, *Poetry Review*, *Tabla Book of New Verse 2001* and *2002*, *Thumbscrew*, *Times Literary Supplement*.

'The Expert' quotes, in italics, two lines of the song 'Corcovado', lyrics by Frederick Eugene John 'Gene' Lees, set to music by Antonio Carlos Jobim and famous from the recording featuring Stan Getz (tenor sax), João Gilberto (voice, guitar) and Astrud Gilberto (voice) (Verve, 1963).

'The Redbeard's Questionnaire' owes its structure and a few of its phrases to 'The Colloquy of the Two Sages', a medieval Irish poem translated by John MacInnes and drawn to my attention by Dr Juliette Wood.

'Valley of Echoes' is indebted to Letter XXXVIII (12 February 1778) in Gilbert White, *The Natural History of Selborne* (ed. Richard Mabey, Penguin Classics 1987).

'The Earliest Days of Scouting' draws biographical details from Tim Jeal, *Baden-Powell* (Hutchinson 1989).

'Against Venice' and 'Our Futurist Theatre' are indebted to *Let's Murder the Moonshine*, selected writings of F.T. Marinetti (ed. R.W. Flint, Sun and Moon Classics 1991).

'L'après-midi d'un faune' draws biographical details from Peter F. Ostvald, *Vaslav Nijinsky: a leap into madness* (Robson Books 1991).

The ten 'Sonnets to Orpheus', after Rainer Maria Rilke, are: I, i; I, iv; II, iv; II, vi; II, xii; II, xv; II, xx; II, xxi; II, xxiii; II, xxix.

'The Nightingale Broadcasts' won 1st prize in the Keats–Shelley Memorial Association's poetry competition, 2001.

'The Breakfast Cup' is based on five lines of a letter written by Elizabeth Bishop to Harold Leeds (15 August 1979; published in *One Art*, her selected letters, ed. Robert Giroux, Pimlico 1996).

Many thanks to Peggy Vance for suggesting the cover image of Japanese cranes and for kindly facilitating its reproduction.

# Contents

## Skywatching

## And How

## The Six-spot Burnet

## Storytelling

# Kyoto Spring Breezes

## The Dragon Gate

By the delinquent, doorbell-ringing,
   trick-or-treating stream
   a scholar who's murdered an examiner

who claimed the year's best student
   as his concubine and failed the rest
   strides along the mossy bank

like a moonwalker with all his library
   on his back, in the first knapsack,
   to a well capped by a giant boulder

where a butcher stores his unsold meat:
   whoever lifts the stone, he smiles,
   may keep the stock, ha ha.

But his grin turns upside down: magic
   is disallowed, and all those flaps
   have marks which must be spells.

An itinerant sandalmaker, hearing
   the cajoling of dogs invited (really?)
   to the fun, runs to try to separate

the pair and finds himself inside
   a six-legged beast all afternoon
   as rank by rank the sun demotes itself

down heaven's ladder, songbirds
   come out of hiding, night falls,
   and before long, supine, shagged out,

staring at the sickle moon, angler's hook
   anathema to all the silvery fish
   of the celestial river,

the three men start to talk –
   of cities built or torn down
   on a whim, good brains in quarantine,

the orchard maps redrawn,
    shoplifters elevated to the round office,
    references weevilled like rice.

No one hears, downstream, the sturgeon
    plop, or knows that just upstream
    is the dragon gate, viewless,

through which, once in a jade moon,
    a dragon thrashes
    out of its sturgeon skin:

*success in examinations.*

# Kyoto Spring Breezes

'Teacher, teacher!' The schoolroom walls are gunmetal grey,
   the ash of February's volcano rubbed to underlying certainty
   of pink by shoulders donkeying with satchels on their way
   to Thrushcross Grange.
                    The cherry blossom cognoscenti,
sipping *sake*, weep to see in this year's blossoms bodied forth
a rice harvest unprecedented in their time,
with rice enough to send to starving distant cousins in the north.

A cherry tree's loose change
                    spilt in the sand is a mime
of the warrior code. The core of self is a cherry stone
locked in a sea of blood. Although the great tit's crime
is knowing all the answers,
                    teacher's likely to condone
such brashness in the flush of youth, garden of flesh
in flower in tints beholden to a diet of bone.
He's seen the kingdom of the dead, like Gilgamesh.

He's heard the moths among the harebells on the heath
   and the soft wind's dances
                    in a monotone
scything the grizzled hair of unquiet sleepers underneath.

# *Tokyo*

Such tricky steps precede the normal fling!
That nurse you might have admired
    has an x-ray
      of your heart and a soft spot, it's said,
      for a sumo welder.

They lie on their backs at cherry viewing,
their sensibilities inspired
    by *ukiyo-e*,
      the floating world of the almost-wed,
      while the earth turns colder.

Those who twirl and those who cling,
the cool and the wired,
    abuzz with the hearsay
      of blood, mooch at the fountain-bed,
      waltz like Matilda.

City without love, there's no such thing.
Our people get so tired
    at the end of the day
      many passengers fall asleep with their head
      on a stranger's shoulder.

## Some Friday Evenings

Every third Friday evening I play chess
with the Emperor one ego-mile above Los Angeles.
We sip mineral water bottled from a spring on Callisto,
synergistic satellite of Jupiter.

The largest thing you'll ever see, pale over Pasadena,
is Taurus the incipient bull with its emotional literacy medal
the Pleiades, one sister without rain-snood in the night.
I need someone who dimly exists, the queening

of the love-pawn Electra, to make myself complete.
Families, like constellations, are a trick of sight.
Some things you'll never witness, bladerunner –

attack-ships on fire off the shoulder of Orion,
mate in five moves, at competition level,
dove escaping, passion breaking, somewhere becoming rain.

## The Shambles

Street names flash blood mischief past your censor.
Beneath the cobbles retch the ghosts of slaughter.
Taxis ply the outskirts, will ride no deeper.
Shambolic dogs nose back towards the Plaza

(smarts of teargas, hops of drunken sailor),
lope round a drunken corner: lo! Copacabana.
I ask about that girl from *Panorama*,
and all you hear's no cowboy's even seen her,

not since the night she gambled with the shaman
and lost the lot: the flat, the cat, her savings.
One asks, then in a moment all's forgotten,

her spirit-flight one-way like notes to Santa,
letters of searchlight love franked Ipanema,
spangled with sand shadowless dreams wear down to.

People in flood: so many brought overnight
from the far hills where they washed and dressed
they have risen, many, to balcony height,

some higher, and a few to the vulture's nest
where they lean upon the cracked guano sill
and scan the town of which they are a guest,

the giant flags, the fires, the general thrill,
petrol set free and running scared in one street,
and in the leafiest quarter the bestial spill

of the zoo enticed by children's trails of meat,
and the trees of The Liberator's Avenue
four lines of stalks, no leaves, so good to eat

for vegetarian beasts, the stripping crew.
Myself, I crave the cool sanctity of cinema,
but it's madness: carnival head, carnival view.

# The Expert

The bathroom was upside-down,
    his and hers in mortal combat,
tornado of two adults on course
    to crash back any moment,
so I ran a hosepipe clamped
    on the hot tap in the kitchen
to an old lion-pawed bathtub
    in the farmyard, enamelled

but badly chipped, and sat on the fence
    and sorted through my plans
while the tub filled, steam
    mingling with the cattle's breath,
and drifted off into my lion's dream
    of Rio – proud Christ
on his 'hunchback', Corcovado,
    swearing to the breadth

of heaven's gate, and all the *cariocas*
    yearning for an expert
to usher them through at a fair price.
    *Quiet nights of quiet stars,*
*quiet chords from my guitar …*
    a saxophone windsailing
me clean over Corcovado.
    But I'd lost track, of course:

the water was scalding,
    though not so high in the tub
I couldn't have tipped in
    two or three buckets of cold
from the cattle trough; and I was mad
    to leave, though not so mad
I couldn't wait for my bath to cool
    in the summer air,

which would have been sound advice
    for the lovers they once were
(I have to assume) – to fill their bath
    from the hot tap, not add
cold, or trouble it with a jug of air,
    just let it cool in nature
to give themselves fifteen minutes
    more in the bedroom.

If you're found cut down, I think we'll all know why.
You're rumoured to have consulted the vampire of Oaxaca.
If so, you'll have been forced to add together the two digits
   of your chronological age to arrive at your spiritual age,
   and then to plot the farewell wave of your life on graph paper,
   the mountain with its seven or eight false summits,
   the jagged blade of the woodsaw.

## My Desert Island

Under the Southern Cross
    lies an island whose history has broken up somehow
    into my bloodstream

like the cargo on the tidefall to the castaway –
    soap, cheeses, kettle, hatchet, dog-paddling home
    along their moonbeam.

***

Under the Southern Cross
    an unfamiliar heat makes language abscond sometimes
    out of its mainstream

into words neither stay-at-home nor native
    – tamarind, benzoar, chachalaca – flattering northern shores
    in their gulfstream.

***

Under the Southern Cross
    the tongue marooned for twenty-eight years of course
    forgets how to swim,

like a dolphin trapped in a tide-cave, songs
    baffled by their own sonic backwash, until the thrashing
    when rescuers stream.

## Ipanema Dreamer

Oh! for a club with bouncers,
tank men with botched tattoos,
    two on the door
    with a Labrador,
and two to patrol the loos,

and two disguised as dancers,
burlier than they seem,
    on the dance deck
    of the friscoteque,
the bulwarks of the dream.

The tariff's gamely liberal,
no charge for the unwaged,
    or the bosun of a craft
    with an overdraft.
There's a crèche for the underaged.

There's a buffet blue with mackerel,
like a chip shop's teaching aid,
    choice cuts of fish
    on an oval dish
in a gourmet marinade.

In Tramps you sense lèse-majesté,
in Rick's Bar déjà vu,
    but the clubbers here
    claim the atmosphere
gives the lie to the bra-hou-hou.

Last night I dreamed of Mandalay
again, at Christmas time.
    Then I dreamed of a bar
    where the advocaat
on the rocks with a splash of lime

runs live in every sailor's veins
and frees their hoard of grief,
   and long-drowned men
   on the deck again
go hurtling towards their reef,

and schoolgirls bright on free champagne
and teachers dark on rum
   wrap practised tongues
   round Bee Gees songs,
and drafts of hee-lee-um,

and the club's called Ipanema,
and it fronts on the Atlantic,
   and they hose your feet
   with a gallon of DEET,
which the barflies find romantic.

Guess I'll always be a dreamer,
and dream of that Shangri-la
   where the bouncers grin
   as they stamp my skin,
'We've been wondering how you are?

'It's a while since you've been in,'
   and the bouncers find
   I've been on their mind,
and they talk to me, blah-blah-blah,
and they smile at me, ha-ha-ha,

   and they're oozing charm
   as they stamp my arm,
and they warm to me, blah-blah-blah,
   oo-la-la, blah-blah-blah,
and they sing to me, la-la-la.

# Valley of Echoes

# The Redbeard's Questionnaire

## A Colloquy of Two Sages

Every lover is a corrective lover.
Every lover is the reproach of limitation.

*A question, instructive lover, how did you get here?*

Not hard to say:
    Along the impatient glasses of my heard,
    Along the milk streams of the milkmaid,
    Along the elfmound of the Joneses' nanny,
    Along the forearm of the ploughman's wife,
    Along the shelves of goodly cheeses
        away from the farm of the sun,
    Along the light of a summer moon,
    Along the fires off the shoulder of Orion,
    Along the green-eyed baby's navel-string,
    Along the green shoots on the branches of old stories.

*A question, well-travelled lover, what is your name?*

Not hard to say:
    Song of passion,
    Passion of fire,
    Fire of speech,
    Speech of knowledge,
    Knowledge of sword,
    Sword of song,
    Grate of ashes in the morning.

*A question, well-named lover, what do you do?*

Not hard to say:
    Stoke subcutaneous fires,
    Immobilise shame,
    Foster poetry,
    Fear and follow fame,
    Parcel knowledge,
    Embroider speech,
    Live in a little room,
    Try to mend broken stories.

*A question, complicated lover, do you have news for us?*

Not hard to say:
    Unwelcome news of the future.
    The cattle of the world will cough all day and night.
    Our finest ploughmen will dream of America.
    Tractors will rust beside the farm track.
    Wealth will not safeguard children.
    Sentries at the dairy will be attacked.
    Housebreakers will crawl under floors.
    Inhospitality will perish the hearthrug.
    Towns will extend into the hills.
    Stammerers will be forced to live together.
    Brawls will take place at heritage sites.
    Horse-dung will show the colours of the rainbow.
    Every skilful person will be proven useless.
    Water will taste of cider.
    Music will fail to mend broken stories.

# Valley of Echoes

*memories of Gilbert White (1720–1793)*

The landscape's folded like your dreams, like your desires –
    may your mother never discover this valley of echoes.

In the hanging woods the cries of a hunting horn,
    the yelps of a pack of hounds, run diminishingly

beyond expectation like a skimmed stone exhausting itself
    while trying to give pleasure to some hopeful apprentice

on the lakeshore. One day a friend of the Reverend White,
    straying far from his companions on a walk, and shouting to

locate them, believed himself to be the target of some mockery
    until, essaying Spanish, French, Italian, German, Latin,

and thinking himself for a minute or two in dialogue
    with the county's one other polyglot, he at last understood

the deception. At midnight, when the air's elastic and
    perfectly still, more syllables might have been elicited,

had the distance home not been too great to render feasible
    any such experiment so late at night, with a new wife waiting.

In fact, the most articulate echo bounces from a building
    or a naked rock, not from a copse ensnaring the rebound.

Best of all was the stone-built, tiled hop-kiln in Galley-lane,
    whose *centrum phonicum* is a spot in the King's-field

on the path to Nore-hill on the lip of the steep bank above
    the hollow cartway where the Reverend White

tested Dr Plot's rule for the articulation of echoes
    (forty yards for the return of each syllable distinctly).

Even a man of the cloth needs no excuse for fascination,
    since echoes touch upon philosophy and mathematics,

even the classics, through the lens of which we learn
   from Virgil of injuriousness to bees, posited

though by no means proven. We'd always understood that insects
   lacked any organ remotely resembling the ear,

though we'd concede that possibly repercussion of sounds
   might tremble somehow through their bodies,

like the ecstasy of love. But how does one explain that
   bees are prosperous here, except when the summer's cold?

The Reverend White once tested their sensibility by shouting
   at hives down a speaking-trumpet, loud enough

to have hailed from Beachy Head a storm-tossed ship
   a mile or so off shore. The bees were unperturbed.

Now, of course, our hop-kiln's dumb – the field between is thick
   with hops, and no one's voice can find its way back home.

# Beatrice in Love

Loudly, the gossips blabbed. She turned up late,
unkempt. Her class ran riot, tossed inkbombs, squawked,
pulled hair. She tried but couldn't concentrate,
her eyes a blackboard where wrong sums were chalked.

Through clouds above her atlas, five miles high,
she saw far countries turn beneath her gaze,
as if the world were round, and rolling by,
and only time could occupy her days.

On pages torn from the register she wrote –
or started – dozens of letters, then like an imp
in a fit of pique she scrunched them up and threw

them at the floor. School was no antidote.
Though even Will Shakespeare acted like a chimp,
why grumble if she played the monkey too?

***

All this the gossips said, for gossip's sake.
Behind the hedge his jaw fell open wide.
A cramp in his pelvis proved he was awake.

Gossip and kindness sometimes coincide.
They feel for her, and so it must be true.
Though sure of being unmarried when he died

(soft-pedalling cynic on life's hard avenue),
that was because he thought he'd die before
he married. Then her passion, like honeydew,

an exudate of angels, made him soar
over purgatorial handlebars,
in orbit, till his touchdown on the shore

of paradise, where she tutored him to parse
the love which moves the sun, and other stars.

## Lud's Church

A chasm roofed with ferns was our assembly room.
Whimsical spiders landed on our skin,
and droplets of week-old rain
pulled by a magnet to their secret pool
like spies called to a conference,
altering course, arriving severally.

We knew the niches where our lamps would stand
arched in their spluttering constellation.
Settling, we felt against our bones
familiar knobbly places, as when
a vagrant husband holidaying at home opens
his arms to the brain-flood of memories.

Damp leaked into our lungs, like the soft wedge
of autumn in the trees. Long-suffering, we sifted
sense from sound, and only then spoke out,
clothing new sense as best we could
around a skeleton of borrowed eloquence,
to drill another soldier for the cause:

*As our lives were treated, so we would treat their laws.*

## The Beaufort Seduction

The sea was like the mirror she'd held
    to my face in play –
which got the whole fandango under way.

She coaxed me to kiss my own reflection,
    then *she* kissed *me* – to prove some wild comparison.

The mirror soon we laid aside,
    our business well
understood. A breeze was blowing now. One ringlet fell,

with a ribbon, followed by some wispy veils.
    There were no foam crests as yet, only ripples, like scales.

I was drowning in the Spice Islands, my dreams less
    outlandish than waking.
The crests were taller, still not breaking.

There was a secret now, trailing a history.
    A few scattered whitecaps flecked the sea,

then before we knew it they were numerous,
    like the cares
only our friends foretell, stealing upon us unawares,

till soon there were many, and later some spray.
    Only innocence keeps intemperance at bay.

The sea heaped up, making me unsteady, likely
    to lurch or lunge
suddenly. I soaked up warnings like a sponge.

Into spindrift broke the edges of the crests.
    I woke up to an image of her breasts,

more intimate than shame. Still, I had reasons –
    meaning excuses.
Only stone men wouldn't have fallen, or recluses.

High waves, and the sea began to roll,
　　dense streaks of foam, my conscience on parole,

my person at risk. Knowledge feeds jealousy,
　　feeding violence
which can boil up even from indifference,

the waves running higher, with crests hanging over,
　　the sea blurring white, so it's hard to manoeuvre.

And this was how my name shrank to a whisper,
　　shrivelled in the heat
a storm will generate from a breeze so indiscreet,

such blinding spray, till the wrong bedroom's right,
　　our truth the only truth, our hurricane a pillowfight.

# The Earliest Days of Scouting

On the little yellow ferry over from Sandbanks Baden-Powell taught
twenty-two boys the word 'spindrift'.
Two or three of them – Lady Rodney's boys perhaps, and certainly
Musgrave Wroughton – already knew 'spendthrift'.

With commendable English stealth over the dew-sodden tents
on the heath to the south of the island crept the pale-faced dawn.
A rabbit in its sand-cave shuddered – feel the tingle in the soles
of your bare feet? – at the cry of the African kudu horn.

Boys tumbled out of their tents to milk and biscuits
and a strenuous half-hour of physical training.
Then came prayers and flag-hoisting – a reprise of the indomitable
spirit their tattered Union Jack had shown at Mafeking.

After breakfast (at eight) there was a mock whale hunt race
between the Ravens and the Curlews,
the whale being a snouted float of tree sawn, carved and smoothed
in a craft guild comprising the two competing crews.

The Bulls and the Wolves learned how to stuff a fern mattress –
in an *envelope* of fern, as one Harrovian Wolf boasted –
and how to mix 'dampers' of dough in their pockets,
later to be wound round sticks at the camp fire and roasted.

There was also a deer hunt, one of the boys volunteering
to be the luckless prey – well, at least it shouldn't be boring.
The 'deer' could climb trees; three tennis balls striking him denoted
the kill, one ball striking a stalker was accounted a fatal goring.

The Poole and Bournemouth boys were taciturn –
all that prissy public school politeness raised their hackles.
Two Etonians watched with mounting incredulous horror
while the Purbeck monster swallowed ten raw cockles.

At seven-thirty came the compulsory rub-down, followed
by a hunter's supper round the great heart of crackling flame.
All around them nightjars whirred and clapped – or goatsuckers,
to use their all too graphic country name.

Then Baden-Powell sang Zulu songs, with lots of
   hard-to-remember, though repeated, vowels and consonants,
and in a kilt of cat-skins and monkey-tails caused
   prodigious mirth performing a rooster-like Zulu dance.

Over nettle tea the camp fell silent as its famous leader
   recounted an adventure of the Matabele campaign.
'When scouting with my native boy near the Matopo Hills
   I spotted some grass that had been freshly trodden down,

'and near by on the track some footprints in the sand,
   small ones, of boys or women, moving toward the scarp
on a long march, as I learned from the sandals
   that they wore, and recent, since the edges were still sharp.

'Then the boy some distance from the track called out
   that he had stumbled across a leaf not native here,
from a tree that grew, oh ten to fifteen miles away.
   This leaf was damp and smelled of Xhosa beer.

'So: a party of women had come from about ten miles back
   with beer – which they tote in pots upon their heads,
the mouth of each pot stoppered with a bunch of leaves.
   Such is the explicatory light intelligent scouting sheds.

'They had passed at four this morning, when a strong wind blew,
   enough to carry a leaf like this yards from the track.
In about an hour they would reach the Matopos, rest awhile,
   then, balancing empty pots on their heads, thirstily amble back.

'The men would want to drink the beer while it was fresh,
   and start upon it straightaway, so if we followed the signs
to their camp we were sure to find them sleepy, guard relaxed,
   and we could reconnoitre safely – behind, as it were, their lines.'

*As I drifted off to sleep that night I thought of an afternoon*
   *when I lay near a little stream in a rocky look-out post.*
*A swish of the tall yellow grass, a tinkle of trinkets –*
   *then suddenly a naked Zulu was standing thirty feet away at most,*

*white tassels on arms and knees, white feathers on brow,*
*offsetting rich brown skin, mock scars of the warpath,*
*wild cat-skins and monkey-tails adangle around his loins,*
*an assegai, a dappled ox-hide shield, a yellow walking-staff,*

*stock-still for almost a minute, like a statue cast in bronze,*
*listening for anything suspicious, then with one quick bound*
*laying his hands upon the rocks and drinking on all fours*
*like an animal, making a thirsty sucking sound,*

*so I could see his lips in my mind's eye touch the water,*
*suck, scarcely a pause, suck pause, enthusiastically.*
*He drank for it seemed an age, rose and picked his weapons up,*
*listened a minute, then moved away, a leaf far from its tree.*

# Against Venice

*after F.T. Marinetti, 8th July 1910*

Old Venice: sick queen who won't abdicate.
In your prime we loved you. Mosquito-blown,
you maunder, centuries past your sell-by date,
rheumatic aches in every crumbling stone.
The waves break up the flotsam of your throne
in a gold haze burned off a sun-scorched sea.
You sink, like a seaweed wreath, with a soft moan
darkwards. Still they drape you in festivity,
soul-pox, lanterns at dawn, love-duel on bended knee.

Your bed has been unsprung by caravans
of lovers. Veiled, they linger a few weeks
round the porch of the Temple of the Glans,
then, crazed, burst in at last, with molten cheeks.
Levantines, Turks, Egyptians, Cockneys, Greeks
crowd the Rialto with the worst of news,
their worm-infected passions and antiques
all counterfeit. St Mark's hypotenuse
tinkles its triangle in adulterous ooze.

Nurses of the saddest sanatorium
in the world, Venetians awake! You doze
in fake moonshine. Dash the ciborium
to the ground, smash all the Doge's windows
to let in the future, scrape the Tiepolos
off the ceiling. Gondoliers, abjure your oars!
Stop digging graves in a swamp. Evolve, dodos!
Cease your rocking-chair rides for cretins and whores
in your beribboned hats and stripy pinafores.

Like the sister of some grand contralto,
Venice, superfluous, reclines inert.
Sound the reveille! Blow the Rialto
sky-high! Sneak a large bomb beneath her skirt
and watch the shadowy queen turn extrovert.
Pave the Cloaca Maxima. A new empire
of electric light dawns. Admit the spurt
of trains, sensuous speed: shock the arriving choir-
master in snow-blue beard and Tyrolean attire.

Venice, don't let those bullies force your nose
underwater – churchmen, poets, dead-eyed
pimps, Ruskin's ghost whose breath can decompose,
the stench of half a million words. This tide
will turn when the hero comes to win you, bride –
brave engineer whose howitzers will plume
your bed, whose giant bridges will bestride
your canals like gymnasts, vaulting from tomb
to tomb in a glitter of knives. Bride, meet your groom.

# Our Futurist Theatre

*after F.T. Marinetti, 1913–1915*

## I

Books are doomed to disappear – like towers,
museums, cathedrals, crenellated walls.
One page puts back the future's birth by hours.

Still worse is theatre, parcelled into cells
like a monastery, moss-grown like an old
abandoned house, echoing with the pratfalls

tragedians make, leaving spectators cold
if they aren't clambering up to snatch a sword
or pistol from an actor, or a purse of gold.

Most tragic are the stultified, the bored –
not those who find themselves some sustenance
in suicide or booty while the rest applaud.

Mannequins weep their toxic effluence.
The final deathcount's five – the audience.

## II

As if, collapsed on the pavement, a horse
gulped down its one last morsel of stale air,
the theatre-goers rattle out in morse

their belch of thanks, hands in a clapped-out prayer
for the soul released from its tale of crime
and punishment, masochistic solitaire,

the stomach from centuries of undigested time.
We've lived our lives in shadow, on parole,
but something stirs along the paradigm,

pumping fresh blood through each arteriole –
a Venus born of smelly estuarine ooze,
her rose brave in the future's buttonhole,

a boxer careless of the blackening bruise,
a fencer skilled in youth's elastic ruse.


III

Like a village waking to a circus troupe,
the cobwebbed stage thrills to the sweeping thrum
of science, a fox delirious in the hencoop.

In the new theatre, war's gymnasium,
Italians smash their dim gas-lamps to bits,
train gymnasts for the hour of maximum

danger, synthesise genius in minutes
in a few flourishes of futuristic grace
like conjurers, for eagles, whelping rabbits –

men who used to stuff worlds of time and space
into the sausage of a single room,
a lying too-many-labelled suitcase

dragged through the sick mind's catacomb
until a new word cleaved the darkness – vroom!


IV

This is the school for a hero's education,
where boys will learn it's madness to denounce
the leap into the furnace of creation

no less than to neglect the planet's governance.
At the Folies-Bergère two years ago
two dancers with a visionary flounce

expounded the diplomacy of the Congo
between Canbon and Kinderlen-Watcheron
in a dazzling symbolic capriccio –

the soul of politics, the birthing swan
whose cygnets are young lads with lordly airs,
each mounted on his winged Bellerophon.

Such a ballet in ten minutes repairs
chronic miscomprehension of foreign affairs.


V


With our actors we've come to fraternise,
valuing their gossip more than Shakespeare.
On sleepless trains with them we improvise,

provoking them to genius – fugitive, sincere –
to the rhythms of the tunnels and the track.
Great artists foam with talent like a weir

small fry can't pass – tireless, amnesiac.
A theatre's fey veil of footlights stonewalls
communication: instead we throw a Cossack-

dance of colour, nets of sensation, the stalls
reflecting red and green onto the stage,
the actors prompted by spectators' caterwauls.

We forge the violent spirit of the age,
the steel of revolution: we engage.

# L'après-midi d'un faune

## Strophe

A Thessaly autumn. No one wears a hat,
because everyone's hair's in love with the breeze.
Far away a waterfall twists its tinsel plait.
A few leaves fall – from the sky, not from the trees.

This world is shallow. Only a few metres wide
at most, but enough for Nijinsky to pose
in profile like a goatish flautist on an urn,

in skin-tight costume, flesh-coloured, pied
café au lait, golden hair and horns, as rows
of nymphs flit past, beside the tinsel burn.

## Antistrophe

Three pairs of cautious flirts, then one alive
with mischief, left behind, whose tricks inflame
the faun as if he'd stumbled on a hive
of bees at his heels frantic to make him lame,

yet still he manages to snatch her scarf before
she slips away, carrying his prize to a rock
where sensuously he lowers himself to touch

his lips on silk, then shudders. Hecklers jeer –
though friends explain this spasm as the shock
of glass grapes breaking in splinters at his crutch.

## Epode

In Chelsea there's a hospice for vagrants
that one day took Nijinsky in, far from well
after partnering six girls in a furious dance
of lust. He'd no English, only his hotel

name scribbled on a corner of cardboard.
Next day the inmates in amazement watched
him clear two rows of beds, doing the splits

above each. One tramp woke as the dancer soared
overhead. Diaghilev, his lover, fetched
him, doling out sovereigns and biscuits.

# The Tomb of Edgar Allan Poe

*after Mallarmé*

Home in eternity, his grasp the equal of his reach,
the poet rallies his century with a naked sword
shaken aloft to flash the news belatedly abroad
that death still shouts us down in harsh, archaic speech.

With a hydra's spasms, a caustic tide the nearest stars
couldn't still, seeing angelic tongues of flame shoot
from his pen, the rabble claimed his alchemy took root
from potions swallowed in demonic rites, or sordid bars.

Clogged with earth, we appeal to heaven – lasting our grief.
If in our loss we've failed to sculpt a fitting bas-relief
with which to decorate Poe's tomb, and make it grand,

let this granite monolith, fragment of glory out of joint,
fall-out of cosmic disaster, as marker to the future stand,
if stand it must – reader, do not blaspheme beyond this point.

# Ten Sonnets to Orpheus

*after Rilke*

## Awakening

A tree grew, like an embryo, as Orpheus cleared his throat
to sing. Its roots coiled through the uninhabitable maze
of the ear. Leaves uncurled from branches, note by note –
a fresh life, beckoning. Slowly, through the morning haze,

animals ventured from their ancient forest runs, shunning
the thicket's subterfuge – till every nest, earth, den, lair
was deserted. If they came so quietly, in the seed-flecked air,
it wasn't that they were shy, or brutishly dumb, or cunning,

it was just that they wanted to listen. Roar, shriek and cry
subsided in their hearts. And whereas before they couldn't lay
claim to so much as a rough hut to offer or receive prayers,

only a wind-thrashed shelter nailed up out of their scares
and cravings, with shuddering birches for an entranceway,
you sang them a temple – a gilded roof beneath a leaden sky.

## Gentle Souls ...

Gentle souls, walk with me sometimes through
the breath of strangers, which parts like rain,
tremblingly brushes your cheeks, then behind you
with a parting tremble joins together again.

Strong, compassionate ones who reach the plateau
of the heart's new capital, settle here, mark
how your arrows love the bull's-eye and the bow,
how tears extend your eyesight through the dark.

Don't be afraid to suffer. Learn to give back
heaviness to the dead weight of the Earth,
its mountains and seas, nothingness to the black

hole inside the Earth's core. Though all the trees
you planted as children now have the girth
of monsters, still there are spaces ... and the breeze.

*To Orpheus*

Oh, everybody knows the animal never existed.
But tell that to the old villagers, who can't stop
loving the beast – its sadness, vulnerable clop
down the lane, long, graceful neck, eyes misted

with gratitude for its sire, their love. Foaled
in a dream-space their woodland moot conceded,
it meekly raised its head. Yes, a thin pulse took hold,
although no milk was to be had. It scarcely needed

to exist. To fatten into life this weakling freeborn
of the heart they'd only to entertain the sheer
possibility of its being, which made it grow so strong

it sprouted a horn on its brow. A single horn.
Later, dazzling white, it soothed away a virgin's fear –
and in her mirror one day answered to your song.


*The Rose*

Rose, we are your coronation. To the ancients
you were a pale cup with a simple rim.
Now to us you are the infinite concordance
of spirit unfolding – *Rosa seriatim*.

In your opulence you seem to be wearing gown
upon gown on a body of nothing but light –
yet each petal separately appears to disown
and dissolve all dress in its endless midnight.

Your fragrance has whispered name after name
to us across the void for centuries.
Again, suddenly, it hangs in the air like fame,

yet still the words escape us. Perhaps we've guessed …
but all we live for is to open our memories
to that sweetness, and the hours it laid to rest.

## Transformations

It's best that we *long* to change, fall in love with the flame
that melts one thing right through to another's core.
Consorting with the sovereign fire we burn off the shame
of struggle, pathetic little flags of the ego's semaphore.

If we shut ourselves up to stay, we'll stiffen before our time.
We're nearest death when we're tense in our own backyard.
Listen: far off, a storm commits an unimpeachable crime,
hammer aloft. The hardest sends its warnings to the hard.

If we pour ourselves like a spring, we'll flow into a wild
country that starts at its innermost frontier, its future leaning
truthfully into its origins; where worry's left its watch behind;

where every new place we reach is the child or grandchild
of our departure; where Daphne, as her fingers, greening,
become laurel leaves, yearns for you to strip down to the wind.


## In the Campagna

You are the unsurprised open mouth in the water-garden,
repeating the one pure phrase of your one true fable,
all those skeins of water bundled into the one cable,
spooling out of your marble mask – my gift, my pardon.

Miles off, aqueducts tilt themselves to their commission
infinitesimally. Towards you down the Apennine slopes
past graves of forgotten loves they bring their deposition.
Syllables abseil from your bearded chin on liquid ropes

into the basin below. Lichen-crusted, chthonic, Greek,
this is the intimate marble ear into which you speak,
lug of the half-sleeping earth mother, always intent

upon her own monologue. I slip a jug under the stream.
She bridles at my saucy interruption to her theme
and, in the change of pitch, voices, mildly, her dissent.

*The Turbot*

From star to star, what emptiness extends!
Here on Earth, between our own lives, greater by far
the distances. Take that child, playing with friends.
How remote from each other even the closest are.

Our fate lies in ourselves, which makes it strange.
Into a silent future we propel our lives.
When a girl fails to meet you at the moated grange,
and hides her love, how alien her motives,

Everywhere distance, the circle incomplete.
The turbot, asymmetrically dead, attends our grace.
How weird its expression on the serving-dish!

Lifted to heaven, white eyes, in mute defeat,
withhold the sea's wisdom – that in a wilder place
we too might mouth inaudibly, like fish.


*Imaginary Gardens*

My heart, sing of the gardens you'll never know,
in the oceanic mind's bottles, safe from dangerous rocks –
Isfahan, where fountains bloom, Shiraz, where roses flow.
Sing of them with joy, in love with their life of paradox.

Prove, heart, that they reciprocate, that their figs swell
for you, that you're intimate with every scented breeze
that petitions from the east, across the farmyard's pigswill
visibly carrying its promise of manure, its aim to please.

Play the tombak and the tar to tell us you don't believe
you're missing something, choosing, like this, to *be*.
Follow the silk thread of yourself in the glorious weave

of flesh, world, moon and star (even if your Book of Hours
feels sometimes like a moment in pain's hagiography).
Beneath each cloudless heaven grows the labyrinth of flowers.

## The Oak Tree

If you summon me at all, summon me to the hour
that always holds you back, that slobbers in your face
like a dog that seems bent on a show of power,
then scampers off on some mad pheremonal chase

when you reappear with the lead in your hand.
What you lose this way is the thing most yours.
We're free. We thought there was a welcome planned
but find ourselves dismissed, excused our chores.

We climb an oak tree, scrambling for a toehold.
Often we feel too young for all that's old
and yet too old for what we never tried.

To praise is the only way we can be sure
of being just. We are the branch, we are the saw.
Sweet danger ripens as our dreams divide.


## In the Small Hours

Silent friend of many distances, feel
how your breath enlarges space. From the dark
rafters of the belfry let the peal
of yourself ring out, each bat become a lark,

singing its exuberance to the harrier.
Be easeful as you turn from shape to shape.
What changed you from a shadow to a warrior?
If the grain tastes bitter, make yourself the grape.

In this tumultuous night flicker as the flame
of magic at the crossroads where every sense
meets every other. Live their confluence.

Don't worry if the night forgets your name.
Affirm to the quiet earth: I flow.
Play to the crowded waters, *pianissimo*.

# The Eel-fare

A transparent willow-leaf the sea tossed
   around the Faroes in 1904: one of millions,
   the fortunate, many more millions lost.
I hatched a dream of tracing a thread
   of ever-diminishing eel larvae
out to some unexpected sea-bed
   where eels whelp in their millions
in fathomless, fecund conspiracy.

When war curtails the study of zoology,
   as with eel studies, animals sometimes
   enjoy a holiday, sometimes flee
from guns in terror of their lives,
   or their habitat's blasted off the map.
Men die in pieces, far from their wives.
   In hunger one might sometimes
grope for an alluringly waisted eel-trap

at night in a mill-leat beside a willow-root,
   poaching like silent death if possible,
   alert for the possible creak of a jackboot
or a huddled sniper's ominous click.
   The fusillade of water-droplets sends
elvers darting every which way in panic.
   Empty! Hunger conjures impossible
doves from a dovecote where the stream wends

past a farmhouse whose black bomb-wound
   is nursed to nothing by the moonlit night.
   The first night we honeymooned
doves like these attended, like bridesmaids
   bribed to stay after the wedding
to loose their soft white cannonades
   of wings upon the peaceful night,
predictive nestlings of the tousled bedding.

Shelling has drained the stream in places
    into underground diversions, but elvers
    find on other elvers' bodies traces
of moisture enough to make a ladder
    of dying comrades clinging to sheer
lock walls up which the slithery armada
    climbs, canal sides tiled with elvers,
scaled with no less ease than waterfall or weir.

For the table, though, one favours the mature
    eel whose yellow has turned to silver,
    a glint of silver in the eye of the epicure
imagining the moonless work at the Po's
    mouth where the catch in a single night
can be a thousand tons, in nets hung to foreclose
    the exodus of contraband silver
smuggling out its gleam, unpacked by searchlight.

Far from the fighting sits the connoisseur.
    If he should happen to receive one day
    after a day a friend spends fishing, as douceur,
a gift of an eel in a bucket, let his thanks
    include his countrymen at the front
in meadows smashed to sludge by rain and tanks
    where reason fights to win, or live, the day,
and men like eels slither in warfare's effluent.

If he's to consummate this thoughtful tribute,
    first he must undress the thing,
    something he's too decent not to fear – uproot
its life from the ground of itself, in a dream
    or fit of madness perform the kill
with a skewer in its head, hang it from a beam,
    peel the glove of skin with pliers, then nothing
for it but the chopping into segments, jerking still.

In 1922 the thread of diminishing larvae
    revealed to me the eastern part,
    the seaweedy part, of the Sargasso Sea
as the spawning ground, inched by the drift
    of continents four thousand miles or more,
straining the instincts of eels by a shift
    that pulls beginnings and endings apart,
then back again by a miracle, like war.

# The Nightingale Broadcasts

Beatrice Harrison, who lived in a remote house in woodland
   south of Oxted, Surrey, was a distinguished cellist.
She was thirty-one when she tried to persuade Lord Reith to sanction
   the BBC's recording, to be broadcast live, of a tryst

she was planning in her garden, with nightingales
   in a copse, accompanied by herself on the cello
playing Elgar, whose favourite soloist she was – if it happened,
   this would be the first ever live outdoor radio

broadcast. In May 1923, on a bench in a sea of bluebells,
   she'd been playing 'Chant Hindou' by Rimsky-Korsakov
when a nightingale had swollen into song 'in thirds,
   and always in tune' with her, from deep in a nearby grove.

It was the following spring, while making her broadcasting debut
   as soloist in Elgar's Cello Concerto with Elgar
conducting, that she'd first hit upon the idea of nightingales singing
   for the nation. Lord Reith supposed they'd be real prima

donnas – costly and unpredictable – and was also chary
   of packaging nature, of making birdsong 'second-hand'.
But Miss Harrison pleaded the case of the poor – all those
   without motorcars, in cities and the north of England.

A rehearsal went well. The broadcast, planned for 19th May,
   would interrupt the Savoy Orpheans' Saturday night dance
music programme just as the Oxted nightingales started
   their evening crescendo. What a performance! –

the summerhouse filled with amplifiers, engineers swarming
   in the undergrowth. Miss Harrison played in a ditch –
Elgar, Dvořák, 'Danny Boy'. Silence. Then, fifteen minutes before
   the station went off the air, a nightingale cadenza, which

gargled and trilled from the oak leaves, flowered through
   a million radios and crystal sets, some of them outdoors,
themselves setting off nightingales, or building in the night air
   a city of song in alien habitats – cornfields, moors,

mountains, housing. For twelve years the BBC broadcast
    Miss Harrison's nightingale concerts (one of them, set up near
a pond, featuring a chorus of frogs). After she moved house,
    the birds were recorded solo, not every year

but certainly in 1942, when engineers captured a nightingale
    outsung but not silenced by a fleet of Lancasters
droning overhead, the first of the 'thousand bomber' raids,
    targeting Cologne, archived though never broadcast.

The RAF had discovered that two out of three bombs dropped
    in night raids on Germany had missed their aim
by more than five miles. Area bombing would be much more
                                                    accurate.
    In the event, both sides turned out to have the same

problem: the average number of days at work lost
    through bombing was only five. Although often
workers' homes were destroyed, morale stayed high: men and women
    still worked, for their country and their distant children.

# A Lecture on Carrots

For my lecture on carrots in the village hall
   I expect an audience split between earth and sky –
   the bent-backed gardeners and the crook-necked
   idolators of flying aces, with possibly a handful of spies
   who've picked up the word 'radar'
   from the ether of conversations that never took place,
   the way a child intuits Daddy's float from death
   while playacting the loss of a Spitfire.

I'll start with the topic on everyone's lips they'll all
   be desperate to gather facts about – the carrot fly,
   notorious for the crops and lives it's wrecked,
   though you'd expect eyesight to be ruined not by flies
   but by, say, firestorms like a violent star-
   birth over Kent, the blinding trace
   of a fellow airman swallowing his last breath
   while hurtling in flames at sea or shire.

The flies are drawn from miles around by the smell
   of crushed foliage, from where, on hatching, their larvae
   tunnel down into the carrot-roots, leaves flecked
   with yellow, a flag which makes us recognise
   we've failed our countrymen at war –
   neglecting to thin the rows, we're in disgrace,
   denying our elders' ways their worth,
   and skimping, like some jobbing hand for hire.

# The Breakfast Cup

*i.m. Elizabeth Bishop (1911–1979)*

My "student" had just left, I was searching irritably in the kitchen
    for his breakfast cup, when I heard through the part-open
    window the long groan of a tractor, maybe two tractors,

grazing the spruces like industrial deer, the annual mow,
    gear changes like the lurching of a plane, the heart
    or hearts in the cockpit freefalling in panic or bravado.

All the bees, hornets, wasps, and blueflies of North Haven
    were gathered up in that drone, though I could see a pair
    of broody iridescent blueflies bouncing above the sill,

where suddenly behind the drape I found the breakfast cup –
    why *put* it there? – then glimpsed a dirt-caked tractor
    cresting the ridge, familiar shock of dirty white hair,

whereupon this thought occurred to me: the old so-and-so,
    eighty a few weeks ago, would not remember what I'd said
    about the cranberry patch, or not till I strode up there,

wiping my hands on my apron. Nor would Dick Bloom,
    who'd brains enough but let his concentration roam
    like a bumblebee from one blowzy thing to another.

Later, they mowed around me as I picked – always keeping
    a neighborly distance, thumbs-up every now and then,
    and young Dick doffing his hat with a grand, sweeping

flourish, as if saluting me in the bank on Main Street –
    to win the admiration of some pretty girl, of course.
    Now I'm making quite a batch of lingonberry sauce.

*North Haven, Maine – August 15, 1979*

# Skywatching

# Snow-watching

At last, a six-toed footprint,
    melting more gigantic still.
The explorer, sampling his aunt's cake,
    bites upon a file.
In the serpentine Great Wall
    of the known world – a stile.

Beyond the farthest fallen
    bone-cairn of the mountain deer
a snow-cliff faces up to gravity,
    like a climber's prayer,
ecumenical at this altitude,
    mutated from a dare.

## Skywatching

After seawatching, the obvious next step.
Ride the blue van, the mobile fabric shop.
Yet how can sky patrols tell where to stop?

Of course, you clock the food-pass or the heist,
but every landing has its friendly ghost.
Pale in the hall, you look straight through your host.

The sea's well managed, a favourite world
entirely trodden by fathoms, like a mould,
whose every mile of fen belies a wold,

and just like earth has features, of a sort –
the play of men, or birds, or depth, or light –
and, best of all, a plane to steady sight,

an eye-chart from the shoreline up, not like
hypnotic clouds on which your gaze gets stuck.
This depth-scale tools, not sabotages, luck.

The sky, all you might love until you look,
blurs you to white-out, lacking depth or mark
to fix that point of song, exultant lark.

## Mountainbiking

To change myself forever takes just a slight
wobble. I tear two or three masts from the fleet,
ground oars, like teeth, lost amid drifts of sleet.

My face was always a tall harbour of shale,
six feet from the bay and rich in sea-coal –
blue lobster's lordly airs in a pilchard shoal.

Most fruit juices give me an unpleasant tang
which makes me feel most of my life is wrong,
kisses of love and thanks wheelclamped, tongue

in a net to ground birds, baited with a moth
that surely as I start dreaming of the south
will turn to love and thanks inside my mouth

again, song-flight appropriately sweet and long,
sea shanty so many voyages till now not sung,
old sail swelled big and loud by unharmed lung.

You minister so well to a waking northern ghost,
heartmeltingly your light dawns in the west.
For the rest of our lives I long to be your guest.

## Mirror Writing

Bad liquorice has got into one upper tooth,
a glancing knock with the rib of the scythe.
For destiny making things half right: a tithe.

My father's pointed out my mother's nurse
claims roots will often capture back their lease,
safe in the coastward footsteps of the Norse,

a scroll of salvage literate on a wreck.
Thanksgiving's in a tavern on the dock,
in an upstairs room: below is Ragnarok.

## The Shaving Tarn

In your kindness you trudge a mile from home
among your family and my friends to a broken farm.
With slops in pails you work against my harm.

Your kids toil as farmhands with you after school,
blooded in the breath of the distempered bull,
unflinchingly peeling red rags from my skull.

Your morning visit brings you over stream and stile
where the ratty rick moults in the froggy pool.
On your back you've a three-legged milking stool.

Red skies flare up around the fractured bone.
What shepherd's bothy lacks a shaving tarn?
There's a dance waiting for us somewhere in a barn.

# The Watershed

His vowels bent eastwards, care-worn, buffed in mink,
a honeybags befriends the frugal whelk,
the bardic he-bear, watering England's milk.

Singers of fifty smokes in a hundred hands,
blunt fingers plough the thickest, foxiest blends
of tea, at dawn, cologning England's hounds.

Far from the census thundering on its drum
he sleeps in leaf-mould watered by the stream,
snug, uncounted, snoring through England's dream.

While the harbour's tomcats and dogs will mount
a scrubbing-brush, or even a ghost of a squint,
his tomcat's AWOL, marking England's mint.

Often he needs the winch to birth some calf,
a tug to yank ashore tidefalls of grief,
in tweeds all night, unmanning England's beef.

His heart's a heath. Soft touch for water-voles,
he's skint, and hauls his sorrow to the hills,
whose only streams flow westwards, into Wales.

# Dr Zeuss

*In the chambers of the Aga*
*  there's a darling squeaky bat.*
*In the pond by the barn*
*  breed the glands that make you fat.*

Dr Zeuss in the Café de Flore
for no good reason starts
on my inner landscape –
the crow-traps, five-barred gates,
rare breeds, wall-eyed dogs,
greased-lightning stoats

of a Cumbrian hill-farm.
Except it's not mine,
it's yours! Somehow he's
flipped midnight and noon,
so your childhood's washed
in the tides of my moon.

*Her bullfrog in the attic*
*for no good reason fails*
*to do what's it's rumoured*
*to be able to, swells*
*but doesn't croak, so where*
*can she hide but the fells?*

*The beck tumbles down,*
*a salmon with blind faith*
*dodging the draft,*
*shy of a cold birth,*
*free of a salmon's calling*
*as it swings into the Firth.*

# Rag

*The boy who made your rug*
*was roped to a loom, gagged.*
Here for him is a *rag,*

a work of cuts to rip
the weave blank in the hope
some news might fret the rope.

We are a heart, a pulse
of words, a blood of rules
spilt on the boards in pools.

We need to find this lad
on his bare plot of bed,
warp his cage, melt his lead,

get him back to his folks
eased of the bruise of rocks
chucked by the warm, sick fox.

*Words are just what you say,*
*the swill of your own sty.*
*Who gains breath when you sigh?*

Not him, not if we fail
to find some yard of wall
our wedge of love makes fall,

fly to the plains to scour
all night his cold, blunt star,
tune his *rag* to our scar,

*make a song of your sleeve,*
*that's all it is, a wave,*
*a gift of sighs to a slave.*

## Finlandia

Melted this form,
    unpaid this debt,
        unsaid
            this charm.

No lost heart's warm.
    After sunset
        drops dread
            of further harm.

Emptying sacks
    and sacrifice,
        hunger implodes
            each honeycomb,

death tax
    of black ice
        on all the roads
            from Rome.

For those who've died
    no earth singing,
        even calling,
            hoists a bloom.

We take pride
    in bringing
        our fallen
            soldiers home.

## Lyre Music

Experienced lovers by moonlight used to meet
    beside the ancient ruin of a lyre
    where Orpheus had buried a dead ox, entire.

Its horns were like a leopard in the hills,
    aggressive long before its leap,
    and brightening as the village fell asleep.

Sawing the end off one horn released bees
    in tens of thousands from a warship
    of liquefied flesh, abuzz with mutinous gossip,

a swarm of nonsense brought to meaning by a queen
    hatched in the spinal cord and brain –
    the judge that passes sentence on the slain.

# La peine forte et dure

It's Christmas dawn.
   Your golem, aglow like a poker,
      resolute, clanking, caped,

knows little of love,
   only enough to have stolen
      to your room while you slept

and slid into your shelves
   his diary in which
      a snowflake's pressed, and kept.

## Fowl, Flesh, Fish

In the bright house of love there's this dark hall
whose lamp is the melt-down of
    a strange fowl
which flies at night from its cave, cries *Sieg Heil!*

and swoops on tree-fruits, blending them into its flesh.
The oilbird, like a dumb owl prized
    for its mush
of pain, fuels us while we prospect for fish

in the bowl of the past, the hopeful sower. Gilled
things abound but shun ants' eggs. In blood run
    black and cold
the fish we dream of flashes – warm, forgetful, gold.

## Glass

Storms flit across the skies of every clone,
iron in the sand that stains old glazing green,
freshening my vow – to keep your windows clean.

Though my ladder's limp, a starter-pack of rungs
loose on the floor, I'd starve to wet-test wings,
hold slow the heartbeat when the doorbell rings.

Sopranos winnow flight from random noise,
silica shoals that baffle roof-high Cs
till a shattering spills our secret: manganese.

Let's learn to fuse our sparkle with our shield,
innocent attics proving their skylights wild,
your throat a crèche, which makes my tongue a child.

## Bathsheba in Love

In this haunted inn we hold
   our most public tryst.
I've just stumbled across the potman
   plaiting sawdust.
For better and worse
   we take our ghosts on trust.

My dress betrayed
   an anguish in the breeze.
Now I'm in travelling clothes.
   Smile? Carouse?
Relax? Catch a weasel
   and shave its eyebrows.

## The Devil's Lighthouse

First some advice for do-it-yourselfers – don't.
Stars are just pinpricks in the latrine tent.
All saints become themselves by accident.

The theatre's dark where torch-bearers have dried.
Upsticks your raindance to the streets instead.
Make shoppers chafe against their clamps of dread.

Tripping and fumbling couldn't matter less.
From damage, like a dolphin, arches grace.
The undetermined moth discovers lace.

# Crimewatch

Napoleon's wines dance on the sundry
main, to the *ancien régime* cry
'Rescue me' in the body's laundry,

some night on an underground coast
feel clean at last – their signatures tossed
overboard. Oblivion absorbs the cost.

*\*\*\**

A roost of tales: fine Sultan's cake
the jackdaw spills like seed, her work
of love to stir dark stars, uncork

the rubied legacy of the Tsars.
From Chaucer's pantry, Shakespeare's cheese.
The Titian only its thief ever sees.

## Night of the Long Knives

The ivy's halfway up the golem's leg,
as if in flight from roiling tides of fog.
Old deeds and wills lie secret in their log.

Gruffly the golem speaks, but only a list
  of names –
the barristers who've ground his wealth to dust.
The owl blinks cagely at the field vole's lust.

To swear the lawyers turned his blood to stone
  defames
them – warranting another dose of ratsbane.
They'll fight his deposition, stain for stain.

And so I fill my bottle at the brook,
moisten the crumbs of my file-tainted cake.
I've miles to go, and promises to break.
I've miles to go, and promises to break.

# Golems Remember

*Just entering Waniewo we heard and saw an ortolan whose leitmotif was loud and bronze, proven among foliage, learned at the eaves of Beethoven.*


A shower admonishes the babbling towers of hay,
clear blue that stamps its mandate through the eye.
Then the rain clears and a sword of sun's held high.

Unthinkingly, young wines cast off their corks.
'Nest' reads as 'nets' in rare surviving books.
Ortolans resign their songs to dynasties of cooks.

Famine of heroic tongues makes even golems grieve,
galvanising fossil lips that mime with love
the cancelled concert in the chestnut grove.

## Samurai Island

For centuries we rough
   islanders have nursed
a grievance – that banished
   from downy breast
we've had to lay a cheek
   on the swan's nest

every night, like a bride
   trapped in a beard
plumped as a pillow
   herself for the swanherd,
at the beck and call
   of his tyrannous bird

ferociously white
   with its angry beak,
its chained neck-collar,
   its withering look,
flown from the pages
   of a storybook.

Our lady of the swan's
   nest, not the lake,
has smacked her lips
   on feasts of eels and pike
she's learned to catch –
   it's hardly ladylike,

but it's a fine way
   to displease her lord,
who wakes to find
   her absent from his bed,
his favourite cygnet
   breakfasting on lead.

## The Good Hearth

Home's aureole lightens here,
deep cave of the hugged bear,
embers in its den, the hair.

Welcome, the other's tang,
incomparable new diphthong
tripped on roots of the tongue.

Free lungs drink mountain air.
High, nimble pamphleteer
whose valley is the ear,

the lag has slipped his leash,
each lid's minute panache
felt larger through the lash.

On loan awhile the lap,
knowing good hearthmanship,
dark stranger on the lip.

# The White Horse

A rider, with halter
  and dismounted grin,
stalks the clearing
  where no horse has been,
unless a white horse
  takes a sleight of green

from the forest, proving
  how a dream's nose
gee'd though the narrow
  wicket of 'unless'
can reach 'if so'
  and pasture in idleness.

A fine horse was asked for –
  paid for, even,
with a quantum of loss,
  the heart's blain
when spurs inflict
  their destiny in vain.

Such trees were the yielding
  ramparts of our life,
and no more masked a love
  than striped a thief –
unless, being outlaws,
  sworn to fierce belief.

If so, you'll see a ransom
  hold a heart in check,
a gambit learned beside
  the greenwood's bark
as the leaves wore thin –
  a stallion, ploughing chalk.

# The Spider

An angel's poison squirted through night skies
sets the heart thumping in a blink of stars.
Tatters of cobwebs are my only scars.

From fusty stables trots the fly-blown foal
whose charm is to forget its sickliest meal.
We cannot *be* the one whose pain we feel,

nor housetrain elders in their muddled socks,
one slipping westward as the other wakes.
But why not love them for each other's sakes?

And why not love the spider like the lamb
whose work is wool, of which your love's a groom?
And why not weave your life-line on its loom?

# The Age of Salmon

*for Peggy*

Your daughter, at four, forages along the Rhine
in a dress pinched out like the corners of an apron,
a bellied sail heavy with hazel nuts and rain.

Your son, at six, swims at the peak of the Thames,
harkening to its tides, its tempers – shaman's drums.
He feasts on salmon mash, with salmon-tasting thumbs.

Red squirrels gather nuts, raiding the dress's folds.
In our golden days of glorious salmon yields
the farmboys muckspread salmon in the fields.

# And How

# Yin Yang

A sailor needs a well
>
> like a miner needs a fountain.

End-on, earth scroll
>
> and water scroll are identical.

Marry a mountain girl
>
> and you marry a mountain.

# And How

Would a stethoscope held where the slick
   chancer cooks his books so the seraph in him twinkles
   register despairs, map robberies in red-cell neighbourhoods?

Would a telescope trained on Orion's cosmic
   short sword shake stooks of stars off the rim of your madrigals
   till shares unstrap their enlightened falsehoods?

Would a misanthrope feel oh no, he'd missed a trick,
   buy Christmas cookbooks, join a fashionable gym, stage musicals
   to endear Astaire's tap to hell-stoked priesthoods?

Would an antelope in the Serengeti flick
   his scut to you, bandy looks with you, grim though the obstacles
   were, make the squares flap, their flares chap, at the likelihoods?

Is the Pope a Catholic? Do one-legged ducks swim in circles?
   Do bears crap in the woods?

## Lost Horizon

I stole a girl in Zanzibar,
    a bed and breast of night,
    a dark trick on her grandpapa.
At dawn she fluttered white,
    a flag and rib of war.

This is the life we understand,
    a horse and heart of hope,
    a long flight in a harsh land.
This is our horoscope:
    a well and mouth of sand.

## Sailors

Your hand on my shoulder, synapse escapade,
   the voltage of undreamed-of possibility,

identical twins in the year of the identity parade,
   each of us a threat to the other's liberty.

## New Moon

No one sees a trained
eye claim this crescent
clipped out of shadow,
pocket and window,
soft, loving name
ajar in its home,
spilt from a bedroom;

and no one stirs
at close whispers
of past and future,
now's long sofa,
quick bright collapse
of heart and lips,
soon or just over,
back in cloud-cover.

So no one knows
how from these fires
the tides that rise
hold off black seas,
bad breeze, high bruise,
or how a thin kite
outside this late,
complete and still,
inside ripens full.

Unsafe
men sleep
in shoes
whose moths
fake rain
to touch

boys, touch
their safe
refrain
of sleep.
Though moths
love shoes,

men's shoes,
skin's touch
lets moths
churn safe
young sleep
to rain,

hot rain
whose shoes
rot sleep,
sour touch.
Unsafe,
such moths,

men's moths,
make rain
unsafe.
Boys' shoes
lose touch
with sleep.

What sleep
can moths
not touch?
What rain,
what shoes,
feel safe?

# The Avatar

When you have your lover
over, she's there to see
your avatar, the true side
you hide or show, the chimpanzee
who upsets the tea,
then armwrestles the Hoover.

She wakes to your disguise,
this cry sunk in your mind,
garret of the trick wave,
sick cave, where she lies upwind
of a frog, thickskinned,
you'd bet she wouldn't kiss twice.

Cock of the Latin Quarter,
you ought to be a big cheese
of being and nothingness.
Wingless you fly, it's a breeze
till you think, then freeze.
Splash! – you're an owl in the water.

You dream she might be cruder,
the mood a delirious mist,
incredible luck like a goal
the whole team scored, not a twist
of an unobserved wrist
by a moth, a munching intruder.

At least your heart's no fake
snowflake – or not exactly –
on a passé sleeve whose charm
oozes harm like a leaking battery.
You've been human latterly –
more than you'd claim for that snake.

## My Grandmother's Dovecote

In the fruity slurry of the flooded orchard floats a dog's corpse
    bloated enough to sail before the wind –
    to my son it's the *Golden Hind*.
So extreme is my misreading of landscape and weather
    I've brought along a tea-tray for sledging on.

Standing (though never walking) arm in arm, we see the graves
    that filled with water as they were dug, and the tower
    where they've stockpiled the fresh dead.
A few snowflakes fall, and a tear, for my grandmother
    two months underground

who lived in a converted dovecote, where one day when we called
    on her for tea she talked of the liberation of Paris;
    of her lover, unable to cycle
in the thronged streets, carrying his bike home through basements
    opened up into a labyrinth

by the guardians of civil defence; of her dovecote, after she moved in,
    haunted by its previous owner who had stumbled
    within a dove or two of starvation –
not only the dead, she assured us, leave their ghosts upon this earth,
    but also many who have *almost* died,

though their spirits are soothed by childbirth, being fond
    of breastmilk, babytalk, lullabies – blarney-eyed nonsense, of course.
    It's the tea-tray that moves you, and my Romanov fake furs.
As I talk of that long-ago, harsh winter
    and a stranger's startling ways with doves –

blunderbuss cricket and the croquet of carnivorous ribs –
    you imagine, having climbed up behind me through the cave-city
    frontage of weather-eaten limestone, undressing me
before a snug log fire, her fine gold chain loosening
    from my neck across your fingers like sand.

# Mood Indigo

A novelist is sick of her husband. Money makes her stay.
They live in the hills east of Seattle in a fine wood
of silver birches resembling the set of a Chekhov play.
The woman and her cousin, a composer, find a mood
that tumbles into sex in a clump of trees one day
during a charity lunch the couple are hosting – a good

thing they're all inside round the piano. There's a good
pianist among them, not gregarious, but she'll stay
if her friend, a nurse, can get everybody in the mood
for music, and if someone really begs her to play
Chopin. The lovers, recovering their breath in the wood,
recognise Polonaise Number 5, which from that day

becomes their tune. For the novelist it's been a day
of miracles, altering her forever. Even so, it's a good
few weeks before she understands it's more than play
the gods have in mind for her – they're in a serious mood.
Perhaps she could make a life with him. He'll stay
in the cold, his music grimly atonal. 'The Birchwood'

is a kettledrum *rag* honouring the trees of the wood
where they first made love. Lasting a whole day,
it starts with an *alap*, a slow prelude to set the mood.
The rest of the piece is a complex *accelerando* you play
with sitar accompaniment. A few buffs think he's a good
composer, though demanding. You need stamina to stay

with this music. Then again, you need stamina to stay
with a selfless man. Now she has a lover – touch wood! –
there opens up from household strain a den of play.
But as time passes the lovers find themselves in a mood
to sort out the future. What if, she says to him one day,
what if I write a book in which I libel you? Good

God, he says, aren't I criticised enough? No, this is good,
she answers. *I* libel, *you* sue and win – *his* money. Stay
ahead of the pack, and we'll take the prize. Bingo. 'Mood
Indigo', goodbye. All we have to do, my sweet, is play
for real. Who would have guessed, that time in the wood,
we'd be pooling ideas together for a plot some day?

Well, even a summer day's too short to think up libels good
enough to stick. 'Mood Indigo', I guess, is here to stay –
the Chekhov play, the moon rising through the birchwood.

## Safe Dreams

Though you cover me safe
with a hat, slice of sleep,
the rain starts with my shoes.
Too late the sight of moths,
holes like rain, another
crime drifted beyond touch.

In their moist park of touch
eyes breasts stroke close and safe.
Droplets on another
pale web divined in sleep
will nourish twilight's moths,
honey to lust of shoes.

Impasse of homeless shoes,
opposites lost in touch,
makes all such fretful moths
blurt out the park's not safe
and we've capsized in sleep –
please wake one another.

Dawn drums up another
strapless wish, to leave shoes
high on the bank, dare sleep
like new clothes, reckless touch
that dreams we might be safe,
bribes us to flit like moths.

I wake remembering moths
that fail, drowned – another
night we'll shepherd them safe
like names on tongues of shoes
or in your bed sworn touch
that lets you sink in sleep,

innocent, neutral sleep
of a ringmaster whose moths
are grounded, out of touch,
while thoughts of another
feel like your high-heeled shoes
in their shoe-box – dry, safe.

Love, when you sleep, be safe.
Waking, touch another
cloud of moths, sky-born shoes.

# The Six-spot Burnet

# A Fox in the Cemetery

Beneath revetted tons of stone, a sleeping corm,
layers uncrumpling in warm rain-fed little springs –
the European angel, northern race, the angel of the storm,
who'll one day wrap these bones in full-grown wings.

A scientist lectured on the twenty types of pain
and won from Darwin and from Darwin's friends
a smattering of warm applause, a freshening rain,
which fed a pamphlet's roots, and almost made amends.

Then mile by mile his map of pain turned red.
He became landscape, imagination flipped on its head,

absorbed into other lives, petrified by local history,
patience and pride, a stone replica angel on show,
like a cormorant far out at sea lifting its wings to dry
in darkening storm-trapped light. The fox left hours ago.

# The Six-spot Burnet

Every flawless day has a present to offer,
like the moth this afternoon in its kimono,
fluttering green forewings, six red spots

on each shoulder, red hindwings, flambeau
of soft fire over our field of knapweed.
The wings beat fast but the flight is slow.

Though lazy and easily taken, the six-spot
burnet is fearless, because full of cyanide.
Every flawless day has a present to offer.

## The Bittern

Shy, fat bird in a forest of brown stalks,
you stretch yourself to heaven tall and lean.
Even a giant so still could not be seen,

no more than could a falcon fast as light.
Safe as only the endangered are,
you intimate close secrets from afar,

mile-off diversions at a fowler's feet.
To know if there's an iceberg in the room,
stop talking. Listen for the foghorn's boom.

## The Kingfisher

How can a bird's pre-conquest iridescent plumage comb
    itself to such a flame of miracle?
    As turquoise burnishes to jade
    at curatorial touch of wintry sun,
    my Christmas present problem's solved in one

to think this kingfisher, hurtling itself into a kingdom
    of resident toys in the free-for-all
    of generations, might dip its blade
    in your first drop of sparkling wine,
    sprinkled across your retina – pretender, flown.

# The Sargasso Owl

Do eels and elvers broil like fish
in a fish farm, or is the view
from a light plane nondescript? –
not a swarm dark and frantic
but a dead zone of Atlantic
your average flying crew
would never think to decrypt

as a lair of eel-flesh, all of this
being just the Empty Quarter
abstract geography. Humped
in a hive of radio, 'Tango, Bravo',
they miss the owl of the Sargasso
a tree's height above the water,
a speck, flapping slowly, plumped

up in its feathers with just enough
energy in reserve to refuel
itself by swooping opportunistically
on a gull. Patrolling a roadstead
of its own making, turning its head –
eyes melancholy more than cruel –
at ninety degrees occasionally,

this owl makes us think, Where can
its nest be found? It's never been seen,
so why believe Herodotus who tells
of a fragile floating bivouac,
a slimy knot of bladderwrack
unravelling as the last of thirteen
owlets fledges amid shards of shells?

# Storytelling

# Lagavulin

I fell from the Cuillin ridge after being taken aback
　　by a fellrunner powering up behind me through the mist.
He shimmied down the scree slope, gave me first aid,
　　then ran four or five miles to the nearest phone box.
Slipped inside my map cover he'd left his business card,
　　*Rory Campbell: Santa, magician, hypnotist.*
A helicopter winched me like a sack of potatoes high
　　above a hundred lonely, glittering lochs.

I'd spent a month on Islay training distillery workers
　　in positive thinking and stress-control,
　　conditioning them to see the annual winter touchdown
　　of 20,000 barnacle geese as a positive relaxation cue.
A leaving party was held in my honour at Laphroaig,
　　with a gig by a gatecrashing storm, a rigmarole
　　of speeches in a hall redolent of salt and seaweed,
　　and a top flight drum-and-bagpipe tattoo.

The consummate team of facial surgeons reshaped
　　my nose, cheeks and jaw, smashed like a windowpane,
　　and patchworked my lacerated tongue, threading its cushions
　　with a single silk stitch, resembling a vein of black blood.
I'd bestowed five lower teeth upon the mountain,
　　redundant offerings to the god of rain,
　　and a world-famous implantologist was flying in to see me
　　in a month or so from Hollywood.

At least I was sleeping well, dreamlessly – I think
　　the surgeons had cured my apnoea
　　by removing and rebuilding my septum.
Sleep was the magic flow country where I felt whole
　　– a landscape bell-like, with beautiful distances,
　　commanded from a peak (Stac Polly, say) by a mountaineer.
Perhaps from one outcrop of rock to the next
　　a mountain goat might execute a nimble capriole.

I turned over in bed, with as broad a smile as my surgery
would allow, and the goat gambolled back again.
But a few weeks later I started waking out of hypnopompic visions –
a mouthful of scree, my jawbone jagged like the Cuillin.
I summoned positive imagery, training myself
to float upon the shore of day within a lifebelt's embrace, a Zen
koan, dry, smoky, peaty malt, its name big, black and blunt
on a sea-washed, whitewashed wall: Lagavulin.

# Storytelling

## Chapter One

In the taproom were five big storytelling armchairs,
   but a satisfying tale was, I admit, rare as gold-dust,
   whether it was the strong ale befuddling the
   autocue

or just that we'd heard it all before – the risks,
   lies, suspicions, discoveries, strikings of camp,
   juggling tricks – till spinning out an
   overdue

resolution right to last orders, frayed beyond repair,
   the storyteller lost us, one fretting about his bike
   with mangled gears, another tuning to an owl's
   hoo woo-woo

from the copse beside Bagg's Farm, remembering
   autumn nights beneath the very tree it roosted in,
   trying not to scare it, moving slow and silent – secret
   rendezvous –

so when they came together it was the owl's hoot
   that blathered of their skill, wild warning cry when finally
   it flung its hundredweight of owl into the night, just as the
   man withdrew.

## Chapter Two

A village asleep in winter always has two lights on
   at least, windows far apart in the huddle of angles,
   on different planes – landlord, a pint of your
   winter brew! –

two yellow portrait frames, or a portrait and a square,
   to warm the throat, a tale of man and woman
   still awake, one counting how many batteries in
   a year two

children's quota of toys will gobble, the other looking
    for a tear in the scrim of the possible,
    Napoleon's summer capital Moscow,
    a rare few

turning marriages inside out and making off with
    their silver lining, but most of us losing
    our daylight altogether, every New Year's midnight's
    Waterloo,

frozen in the snow outside the Fox and Hounds,
    while New Year revellers notice merely
    that someone seems to have slipped away, into the
    midnight blue.

# *Erratics*

## One

Unimaginably ancient stones carried off by a glacier
　　on a topographical adventure fetch up in turnip fields,
　　a nuisance.

Prisoners break them, cart them, making friends under their breath,
　　heads down, frozen in hempen clothing, sullen under
　　surveillance.

Market-town cobbles massage soles of tourists' feet inexpertly,
　　prompting retreat off the street to a snug where over
　　cups of gin

four locals leaning towards a two-bar fire in a ghost
　　of eau-de-nil and fluted glass turn to stare, as if we had let
　　the ice age in.

## Two

In food riots once, when likely-looking missiles, firmly cemented,
　　resisted a gang's work with posthammers to make
　　them feral,

these rioters, not flinging posthammers themselves
　　to break important windows, must have been inhibited
　　by a scruple,

aptness of cobble for the hand, in the scale of conscience
　　weighing little more than the hand itself plus an increment
　　of showing,

as if heroic acts must fall within the circle of the self,
　　like diving to prevent a drowning, instead of casting off a boat
　　and rowing.

## Three

If a malachite egg in our bathroom yearned to nestle in my palm,
　　ambassador's cushions of flesh, who would not try
　　to be equal

to such desire, not souvenir nor monument, but fuel of touch,
　　romantic trajectory, beyond scrimmage, stumble and fall –
　　my sequel.

Tundra's renewal flowers through ice to great applause,
　　as the fragile egg survives sod's law's hammer, egg-collectors,
　　skua's hunger,

mercury clambering up at dawn to the big thaw,
　　avalanche of stones, each stone highstepping by to leave me
　　safer, younger.

# Bottomfishing

*Too few otters, too many mink: otterhounds were bred*
*to a new calling after otterhunting was outlawed in 1975.*


I'm bottomfishing in the gloom
of the global share collapse – Dow warrior.
The heck if I can quite see what I'm doing.

I'm mothballing equities like mink
of a more glittering, tarnishable era –
mink with a distinct Park Avenue scent

by way of Wall Street. Sexual mink.
I'm master of our minkhound pack
and four times winner of the songfest

thousand-guinea purse – this year
the Ytene Hunt, sad blighters,
never knew what the devil hit them.

                    ***


Last month at Culmstock another mink
attacked another fishing competition.
The toll was fifty keepnets wrecked

and half as many top-of-the-range rods
the anglers used to try to prod or flick
the beggar back into the water.

The Fox next lunchtime was aheave
with pressmen and loss adjusters
only doing their jobs but playing merry hell

with the Culmstock mink pack meet –
three-deep at the bar, injury time,
last orders soon to sound its morbid knell.

                    ***

A fight broke out between contenders
for the last ploughman's, as if it were
St Petersburg's one remaining hank

of month-old mink from the former
Park of Soviet Economic Achievement,
worth every rouble of a lifetime's savings.

A darts player was thrown against a wall, and
then it seemed for a damn destiny-defying
second that the trophy case might stay

aloof from chaos on a crest of self-belief –
until the otter muffed its unexpected
longed-for final dive amidst a splash of glass.

# *Aux armes, citoyens!*

As from today baptism is again the right of every citizen.
Each warlord must promptly drain the moat around his castle.
Only king or queen may sequester the well of any citizen.
The queen is godmother to every child, the king owns every horse.
But one day a horseman in mud-spattered black, reluctant citizen
of the laws of nature, canters along the river-bank. Purple
willlowherb shields me as I watch in amazement this citizen
unfurl my secrets on a long, looping banner. Clothes my mother
wore in church last week lie strewn like lovers at rest, the citizen
naked by the river, my mother in underthings. He knows my father,
but resents him and is pleased to do him harm, like any citizen.
He has unforgettable bruises my mother bathes tenderly – purple,
yellow, black, like an orchid, unregistered armorial of a citizen
locked in a tower all night, in the morning dragged by a horse
by his heels round the yard through the slops of our banquet, citizen
of a ghetto of pain. His treasonable passion is both siege and castle.

A ghost at the baths, I have abandoned my watch at the castle.
Waist-high in the thermal pool I play fading chess with a citizen
of this town, a stranger, Gentile – strong and silent as a horse.
Only secret police may plant a microphone on any citizen.
Up at the castle a woman receives dye of forbidden purple
in a snuff box by moonlight. The Danube winks. My citizen
of Buda loses his queen – he is old enough to be my father.
Young men circle me slyly, seeking eye contact. One citizen
has brought a fabulous set in ivory, a gift from his mother.
A sumptuous present may be the undoing of a good citizen.
I check the pieces for secret microphones, frisk the purple
velvet lining of the box. He is Jewish, this strange citizen.
He twists by its stern rider's plumed helmet first the one horse,
then the other, to face the enemy. *Aux armes, citoyens!*
Each rook is an elephant, immovable, its saddle a small castle.
Each bishop is a theologian. Each pawn is a famous citizen.

## The Stables

Where the stables stand
and the palace is destroyed,
there'll be haunting
by neither people nor horses.

History's placebo is porcelain,
the monkey orchestra and,
coarsely poignant
in their fragility, the roses.

Cryptic in this habitat,
one in a hundred might concede
molecular dust of ostlers,
soot-shadows of nurses.

Though my daughter borrows
silence effectively,
shuts herself away at midnight
with the sources,

soft blur of hands
is more than anyone expects
from so dreamless a place,
let alone faces.

# Drovers

A sailor's son, marooned in a fishing port – Jesus! A friend
one day, feeling the law closing in, said why not wing it south
together down the drovers' road? Snuggling at night with cows
we'd never be short of excitement. Did I have decent shoes
or, better still, clogs? He could sell me some – remember
he'd knocked off the quayside stores. I'd make a fine drover,

properly kitted out you'd even think I was a *born* drover.
Oh yes, here for your long woollen leggings take, my friend,
this outer pair of leggings of brown paper. Remember
to waterproof the wool with soap, and don't think south
is where palm trees grow. If you see anybody without shoes,
they're poor as pigs. To find out more, just ask the cows.

So we sat by the tree on Trump Hill till a herd of cows
came snaking down the lane, tailed by a dog and their drover,
then we ran down and offered our services – two pairs of shoes
to trot ahead and flush out a robbers' ambush, tell friend
from foe, fight hard or be good company all the way south
to London, where we'd vanish on demand. Now, remember

these were violent times and, something else to remember,
he probably durstn't say no. So we fell into step with the cows,
their collie and their man, and trekked some twenty miles south
each day, overnighting at inns but living on scraps. The drover
I got to know well, he was gentle and quiet, and a friend
to anyone who'd swear at him with a smile. No one in his shoes

could have matched him for humour – even after those shoes
had bellyflopped in a spate of mud. I'll always remember
his courage too – in quicksands, rescuing his old friend
the ferryman from a freak tide, swimming with the cows,
hanging on to their tails, and dodging the toll, as any drover
would, but one that had us swinging off the high road south

to scramble down a loose slope of scree, then turning south
again shy of a yard of skin in lieu of cash, with ruined shoes.
The rains bollocksed us like that tidal wave. Who'd be a drover,
I thought, as the sleet came pelting down. To remember
the sun brings no warmth – all weather's now. The cows
looked sick, the drover looked worse, even my tough friend

on the run was sneezing as we pushed on south. My other friend
the drover died beside a blacksmith's forge. To remember
him I pocketed one of those curious cloven shoes for cows.

On distant farms where brawns are bred
    we quislings learn to quench our qualms.
We breakfast royally, in bed,
        at ease on distant farms.

The good life snakes its ample charms
    through all that's thought and all that's said.
At beggar-my-dog The Weightwatcher's Arms

annihilates The Angler's Head.
    To the faint music of distant alarms
we ruminate, ill-kempt, well-fed,
        at ease on distant farms.

***

In shepherd's caves, redemption-hound,
    we shelter while the shepherd shaves,
hoping our luck won't turn around,
        happy in shepherd's caves.

Our shepherd, like an angel, braves
    a scything flood that wakes his wound.
At blast-my-soul The Prince of Graves

humiliates The Nymph Aground.
    We sing amid the worsening waves,
safe and dry where sheep have drowned,
        happy in shepherd's caves.

***

On windless fells in bowls of scree
    we yodellers yomp our yearning yells
from crag to crag, exhausted, free,
        walking on windless fells.

We hump in fields of asphodels,
    declaring our love belatedly.
At jolly-my-gum The Cockleshells

eliminates The Milking Tree.
      Our water comes from streams, not wells,
and keeps our spirits up, like tea,
         walking on windless fells.

          \*\*\*

Above the bay, wave-lashing rocks,
      the west wind leads our wits astray,
like wayward stragglers from flocks
      of gulls above the bay

where, ten to the dozen, dolphins play,
      maddened by the equinox.
At slack-man's-pride The Old Cathay

exterminates The Wily Fox.
      We've given our worldly goods away,
exchanging wives and quilts and clocks
      for gulls above the bay.

          \*\*\*

Out in the straits a holy mill
      of light through noise of night pulsates
to flash the news, we're praying still,
         on our rock out in the straits.

One lighthouse now accommodates
      the city of God, and does God's will.
At dibble-my-dock The William Gates

embarrasses The Shepherdess.
      Our treadwheel groaningly rotates
to strip of its perilous black dress
         our rock out in the straits.

# Umbrella in a Briefcase

*'No one's suggesting we put the rain back into the sky.'*

Umbrella in a briefcase,
   precipitate through the city,
   folded lungs in a high-risk drowning zone.

Your goal is to be in great shape for the meeting,
   powder dry when the time comes
   to foist aloft your dream.

Your dream is to breathe yourself into control,
   distil innocence,
   eyes resourcing the future.

Your purpose is to be at work, awake, ahoy,
   when the gooks sail by
   to pilfer the dew.

# Wanted

Some wishful cuckoo freaks the gentle West,
this hearth of sexual heat wild menfolk spurn.
All cowboys long to torch their secret nest.

The kids are feral, thoughtful, self-possessed,
womenfolk, weeping, watch their wagons burn.
Some wishful cuckoo freaks the gentle West.

The Crippen gang are riding six abreast
but stop for beans, a mustang at their stern.
All cowboys long to torch their secret nest.

The fireflies – dudes! – spangle your fancy vest,
strong coffee lowers the stars, tin stomachs churn.
Some wishful cuckoo freaks the gentle West.

Sioux on a ridge, affronted, unimpressed,
yank at the reins to make their horses turn.
All cowboys long to torch their secret nest.

I've heard the bounty robber's last request
was an English breakfast: such men never learn.
Some wishful cuckoo freaks the gentle West.
All cowboys long to torch their secret nest.

# Baroque Rectangular Mirror

### Top (short) side

The once-in-a-while change of watch,
we know and trust each other,

and we're serious, ready to be
hero of the scheme of things,

yet nobody's invented playback yet,
whoa, Quicksilver Valley, forget it,

memory is curious yet obedient, eyes closed, in a corner, counting,
even if right in the middle of the important wall of the room.


### Right (long) side

Over weeds, or homing eels, rippling over an ocean shelf, on our
dark side,
contrariwise such shoals of anxious silvery fish flash by, as if startled,

like kittiwakes by a great skua, by a frogman homing towards a
barnacle bomb
clamped to a liner's hull, while dancers above in their hundreds

swoop and skirl in the hall of mirrors, gambling blindly on a polka
in lieu of a prayer, white flounces abandoning the floor in frantic
synchronicity.


### Left (long) side

Windless re-gildings, dusting of hollows, ostrich feather's dutiful care:
mist-nets for ghosts no longer spry, like fierce janitors of
unfashionable spas,

not bothering to make themselves scarce, retained among acid
shadows,
shells and volutes crumbling where the grotto greenly drips,
Bathe here,

they recommend, This water's mineral-rich, stay till you feel the rub
of whorled dunes on your fingertips, feast your spirit on the food of
time.


### Bottom (short) side

You ask why we discourage eyebrows, prefer brush-arches
a fraction-inch higher, broader, as if you didn't know

surprise can be exquisite spun
through all the hours of social fray,

yet you imagine over the crest
of our bare shoulders mirror dawns,

desire in the vulgate while our helpers and
our hounds lie still asleep.

## Second Copies

My second copies of my best-loved books –
the ones I travel with and annotate,
stuff into rucksacks or pub's inglenooks,
dash off with on some swamp-infested date –

trail in their margins an idea or two,
a thought-snail careless of its glistening track,
on the roadside verge a picnic's residue,
a wishbone floated off a space-walk snack.

A clone may turn out hardier than its stem,
more daring and more talkative. Wise heart
of birth or marriage song, or requiem,
drives fast and true the righted applecart,

cracking its whiplash just beyond its words.
Good books are riddled like a honeycomb,
all spaces and solids, windblown, like the Kurds,
and wisest in the desert, which is home.

# Alabaster Casket

*Too late to find fresh air not rationed like this?*

**The sandwiches**

Johndo,
   there's a plan to muster in the Half Moon again
   on the shady corner opposite the Market
   within the beer-soaked lee of St Mary's Church
   where Lord Byron's heart withers as intended
   in its alabaster casket.

Since Christmas
   I've been camping alone in my uncle's flat,
   drilling his inexhaustible memorabilia
   into my regiment of cardboard boxes and A4 plastic wallets,
   living on supermarket sandwiches which seem to start swarming
   with biological defeat the moment I bring them upstairs,
   even before their seal is broken.

Bread hardens
   in front of my eyes, and I swear a white speck of mould
   stepped forward just now from the wholemeal jumble,
   a lone volunteer for the dirtiest duty:

someone has to do it.


**The calendar**

New corridors
   in space transecting layers of time unearth exhibits
   of our past incredibly restored, as if by the Rialto multiplex
   a child, power-crazed, had ploughed this alleyway
   from which, as from sparse bubbles of drowned love,
   I breathe again the TV workshop, Stefan's language lab.

How lucky if
    I live to see the last flake of old maroon paint
    peel free, like the monthly turn of the girlie calendar
    whose furtive chaperones stood machine-faced
    in their conspiracy, their tinkering done,
    their talk like swallows dipping round my head,
    the wives back home in league with forces' sweethearts
    in their knowing smile.

Around seven
    my uncle turned up, doled out the pay packets,
    and money's grin backwashed up the bloodstream
    where we'd left our clothes on the bank –

swimming to disguise our lameness.

In Skibo Castle a film-maker, Guy Ritchie,
   and an actress/rock star,
Madonna, married yesterday in a whirl
   of Scotch mist. The press
were expertly shut out, despite
   the enormous budget for dirty tricks
the tabloids commanded. The day before
   was the baptism of their son
Rocco. Two men with a camcorder squatted
   for more than sixty hours
in the organ of Dornoch Cathedral
   with bin liners to piss and crap

in, astronauts of the stratosphere of
   info-tainment, choosing a crap
way to spend the party season, pinning
   donkeys' tails to a star,
but happy in their grumbling even
   during the deafening two hours'
torture of the organ rehearsal the previous day –
   what a story to impress
the tattooed lassies they meet at dances.
   Being so far above Earth the Sun
's never hidden, these astronauts know God
   by rumbling his best tricks.

As I hide in the *Observer* from my mother,
   some of God's tricks,
I can't help thinking, aren't worth
   a cut-price Woolworth's crap-
scented candle, like the memory trick
   that asks a volunteer, her son,
to write on a slip of paper 'water infection',
   naming the puckish star
that has my father helping her on and off
   the commode all day. Press
her, you'll find it's fear, not nature, calls.
   This sadness fills their hours,